PRIMARY SOURCES

★★★★★★★★★★★★★★★★ OF ★★★★★★★★★★★★★★★★
IMMIGRATION AND MIGRATION
★ IN AMERICA ★

IMMIGRANTS IN COLONIAL AMERICA

Tracee Sioux

The Rosen Publishing Group's

PowerKids Press™
PRIMARY SOURCE

New York

To Ainsley Sarah Thornton, my reason for having a day

Published in 2004 by The Rosen Publishing Group, Inc.
29 East 21st Street, New York, NY 10010

First Edition

Editor: Rachel O'Connor
Designer: Emily Muschinske

Photo Credits: Cover, pp. 7 (top), 19 (top) © Bettmann/Corbis; p. 5 Library of Congress Geography and Map Division; p. 7 (left) © Nik Wheeler/Corbis; p. 7 (right) courtesy of Map Division, The New York Public Library, Astor, Lenox & Tilden Foundations; pp. 8 (top), 12 (top), 16 (top), 19 (bottom) © Hulton/Archive/Getty Images; p. 8 (bottom) © Christie's Images/Corbis; p.11 The New York Public Library/Art Resource, N.Y.; p.12 (bottom) © Richard T. Nowitz/Corbis; p. 15 (top and center) © North Wind Picture Archives; p. 15 (bottom) Picture Collection, The Branch Libraries, New York Public Library; p. 16 (bottom) © Burstein Collection/Corbis; p. 20 Culver Pictures.

Sioux, Tracee.
Immigrants in colonial America / Tracee Sioux.— 1st ed.
    v. cm. — (Primary sources of immigration and migration in America)
Includes bibliographical references and index.
Contents: In search of a better life — The first immigrants — Religion in the colonies — The native Americans — The southern colonies — Slavery and indentured servants — New England colonies — Government in the colonies — The middle colonies — Today's immigrants.
ISBN 0-8239-6823-5 (lib. bdg.) — ISBN 0-8239-8949-6 (pbk.)
1. United States—History—Colonial period, ca. 1600–1775—Juvenile literature. 2. Immigrants—United States—History—Juvenile literature. 3. Colonists—United States—History—Juvenile literature. 4. United States—Social conditions—To 1865—Juvenile literature. 5. United States—Emigration and immigration—History—Juvenile literature. [1. United States—History—Colonial period, ca. 1600–1755. 2. Immigrants—United States—History. 3. Colonists. 4. United States—Social conditions—To 1865. 5. United States—Emigration and immigration—History.] I. Title. II. Series.
E188 .S615 2004
973.2—dc21
                              2002153315

Manufactured in the United States of America

Contents

A New & Correct MAP of the

WHOLE WORLD

Shewing ye Situation of its Principall Parts. Viz the
Seas, Kingdoms, Rivers, Capes, Ports, Mountains,
Woods, Trade-Winds, Monsoons, Variation of ye Com-
pass, Climates, &c.

By HERMAN MOLL Geographer. 1719.

In Search of a Better Life

Every person who lives in America today is either an immigrant or a descendant of immigrants. Even the Native Americans are immigrants. They came to America from Asia thousands of years ago. After Christopher Columbus had explored America in the late fifteenth century, immigrants began to arrive from all over Europe. They came from places such as Spain, England, and France. They came in search of a better life, free from religious and political persecution. They hoped to find wealth in the land's resources. After the immigrants arrived, they began to establish settlements known as colonies.

A world map from 1719 shows that parts of the Midwest and the West of North America had yet to be explored. By the mid-1700s, there were approximately 1,600,000 immigrants in the 13 colonies on the East Coast.

The Immigrants Establish Colonies

The Spanish were the first to establish a permanent European colony in North America. They settled in St. Augustine, today's Florida, in 1565. However, it was the British who later founded many of the colonies. In 1607, the British set up their first colony in Jamestown, Virginia. The Pilgrims then founded Plymouth, Massachusetts, after arriving on the *Mayflower* in 1620. In 1626, Dutch settlers bought New Amsterdam from Native Americans. The British later took over this colony, naming it New York. By the early 1700s, the British controlled the East Coast and had established 13 colonies there.

Spanish colonists built the watchtowers of Castillo de San Marcos, in the early 1700s, to protect the town of St. Augustine. During this period, the Spanish also had colonies in South America, Europe, Africa, and Asia.

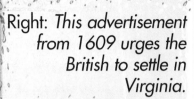

Right: *This advertisement from 1609 urges the British to settle in Virginia.*

Above: *Jamestown was the first of the 13 original colonies to be settled, in 1607. Georgia was the last, in 1733.*

Above: *The Spanish Armada, consisting of about 130 ships and 30,000 men, was defeated by the English on August 8, 1588, after several days of battle.*

Right: *James I, king of England, reigned from 1603 to 1625. He belonged to the Anglican Church and made life hard for any non-Anglican subjects.*

Religion in the Colonies

One of the reasons the Europeans flocked to America was religion. In 1588, Great Britain's defeat of the Spanish Armada, or navy, resulted in Britain becoming the most powerful force in Europe. A period of religious unrest followed. The British rulers told their subjects which church to follow. The Pilgrims, who arrived in New England in 1620, were the first group of immigrants to come to America to escape religious persecution in Britain. They were fleeing King James I, who would not recognize their religion. The Puritans also came to Massachusetts to escape persecution in Britain. Pennsylvania, which was colonized in 1682, became a safe place for another large religious group, the Quakers.

The Native Americans

Immigrants came to America dreaming of wealth. They hoped to find gold as the Spanish had in South America. Instead, they found vast amounts of land populated by Native Americans. The Indian nations reacted in different ways to the European settlers. Some were helpful, teaching the immigrants how to farm the land. Others were not so friendly. The Native Americans in Jamestown met the immigrants with hostility. The Indians feared losing the land on which they had settled, and they attacked the colonists. In the end, however, the newcomers forced the Native Americans to leave.

This late-sixteenth-century engraving of an Indian settlement on Roanoke Island, now part of Virginia, shows how advanced and self-sufficient the Native Americans were before the British immigrants forced them to leave.

Shortly after the British immigrants landed in Jamestown in 1607, they had to build a wooden fort to protect themselves from the Algonquian peoples.

Jamestown was the first colony where tobacco was grown as a cash crop.

The Southern Colonies

The first European immigrants, who had settled in Virginia, had come looking for gold. Instead, they discovered land that could be cultivated to produce tobacco and other cash crops, such as rice. At first the colonists in the South were not interested in cultivating the land. They wanted to get rich quickly. Working the land was too hard and would take too long. To ensure the survival of the colony, a man named John Smith stepped in and took control. He made the immigrants work the land. It took longer to make money by raising crops than by discovering gold, but the land provided the immigrants with the opportunity for great wealth. In the 1600s, many colonists started to build plantations.

Slavery and Indentured Servants

The colonists in the South found that there were not enough people to work the land. One remedy was to bring black slaves from Africa. These people were forced from their homes and were made to work without pay. Slavery began in America with the arrival of 20 slaves in Jamestown in 1619. The use of slaves continued to grow throughout the colonies. By 1790, there were 300,000 black slaves in Virginia alone. Indentured servants were another remedy to the labor problem. Indentured servants usually traded three or four years of hard labor for their passage to America. At the end of their term, they were freed. Some indentured servants were given land of their own to farm.

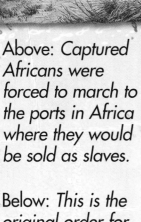

Above: Captured Africans were forced to march to the ports in Africa where they would be sold as slaves.

Below: This is the original order for the sale of an enslaved African boy in New England in 1761.

Above: When they landed in America, the Africans were sold at auction, where they were handled like animals.

To Mr Samuel Jones in Bolton in the County of hartford Thefe are to defyre you to Sell My Negro Boy Named here about 13 years old att all boy to the Beft advantage you Can But Not to Sell him Cafe you Cant get forty pounds lawfull Money for him Colchester august 5th 1761 Oliver Bulkley

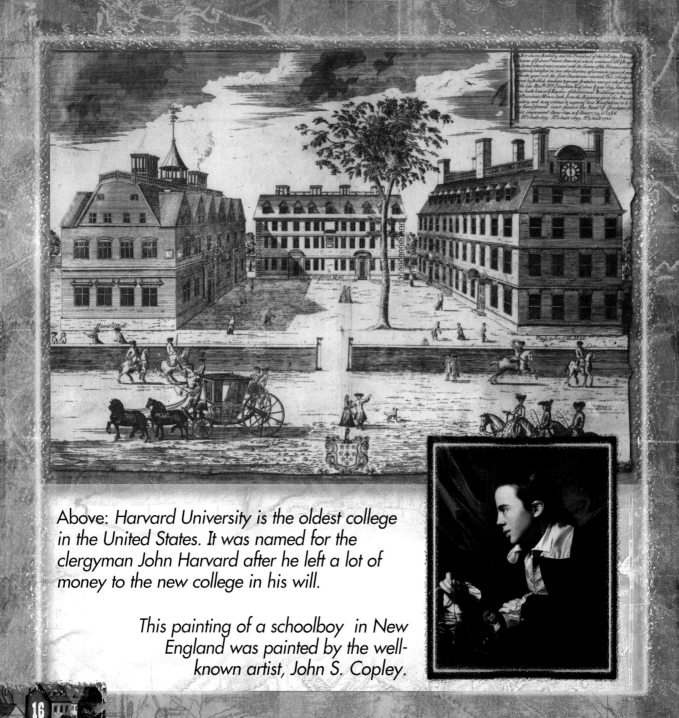

Above: *Harvard University is the oldest college in the United States. It was named for the clergyman John Harvard after he left a lot of money to the new college in his will.*

This painting of a schoolboy in New England was painted by the well-known artist, John S. Copley.

New England Colonies

Unlike the land in the southern colonies, the land in northern New England was not very productive. The soil was thin and stony, unsuitable for farming. Many of the immigrants became fishermen and sailors. They settled in areas around the harbors. The towns that grew around these harbors became important centers for business and trade. Education was also important in New England. One law ordered that a school be established in every township of 50 families and that an elementary school be built in the larger towns. Boston Latin School was founded in 1635. It was the first public school in America. In 1636, Harvard was founded in Cambridge, Massachusetts, then called Newtown.

Government in the Colonies

Before the Pilgrims even landed in Plymouth, they had agreed on a system of government. On November 11, 1620, 41 men signed the Mayflower Compact. The main idea of this agreement was that the people would vote on the government and laws, accepting whatever the majority chose. This is one of the first examples of majority rule. The colonies were supposed to be governed by Britain. However, Britain was busy in wars with France and Spain, so the colonies mostly developed their own laws. All colonies agreed to follow the Magna Carta, a British law that assured basic rights to every individual.

All 41 men on board the Mayflower *signed the Mayflower Compact as the ship was docked in Cape Cod harbor.* Bottom: *Here are some of the names of the people who signed the original document.*

John Winslow

Thomas Cushman

Nathaniell Morton

tho: Prence

john Bradford

consbut Southworth

William Bradford

Tho: Southworth

Edw: Winslow

Willm Brewster

Myles Standish

Isaac Allerton

The Middle Colonies

The middle colonies had a greater mix of immigrants than did the New England or southern colonies. This was perhaps because the immigrants here practiced more religious tolerance. The Dutch were among the first immigrants to come to the middle colonies, settling in New York. By 1646, New York had a huge cultural mix. The settlers included the English, Scots, Irish, Dutch, Danes, Norwegians, French, Poles, Germans, and Italians. Pennsylvania, another middle colony, was founded in 1681 by William Penn. It became a safe place for the Quakers and others seeking religious freedom.

This picture, called On the River Front, *shows a busy street scene in New York City when it was the Dutch colony of New Amsterdam.*

Today's Immigrants

By 1700, there were 250,000 immigrants in the 13 colonies. This number doubled every 25 years until 1775, when there were more than two million people on the East Coast of North America. The level of immigration increased or decreased depending on the quality of life in Europe, and, later, in other parts of the world. Today immigrants continue to arrive from all over the world to settle in the United States. Just like their ancestors, they are in search of a better life, a life free from persecution. The arrival of people from so many different cultures since the early seventeenth century has made America the democratic society that it is today. Mostly, it is a society that tries to embrace difference.

Glossary

ancestors (AN-ses-terz) Relatives who lived long ago.

cultivated (KUL-tih-vayt-ed) Grew, as in, cultivated vegetables.

cultural (KUL-chuh-rul) Having to do with the practices, arts, and beliefs of a group of people.

democratic (deh-muh-KRA-tik) In favor of democracy, a system in which people choose their leaders.

descendant (dih-SEN-dent) A person who is born of a certain family or group.

developed (dih-VEH-lupt) Worked out in great detail.

immigrant (IH-muh-grint) A person who moves to a new country from another country.

indentured servants (in-DEN-churd SER-vints) People who have worked for another person for a fixed amount of time for payment of travel or living costs.

permanent (PER-muh-nint) Lasting forever.

persecution (per-sih-KYOO-shun) The act of attacking because of one's race or beliefs.

plantations (plan-TAY-shunz) Large farms where crops were grown.

reacted (ree-AKT-ed) Acted because something happened.

resources (REE-sors-es) Things that occur in nature and that can be used or sold, such as gold, coal, or wool.

survival (sur-VY-val) Staying alive.

tolerance (TAH-ler-ens) Acceptance of other people's differences.

Index

Primary Sources

Cover, title page. Inset. Advertising America to Englishmen in 1609. From the London Company pamphlet "Nova Britannia," this advertisement is looking for colonists to come and settle in Virginia. **Page 4.** 1719 map of the world by Henry Moll. **Page 7. Left.** Watchtowers of Castillo de San Marcos. Built 300 years ago, this national monument still stands, overlooking the Atlantic Ocean in Florida. It was built to protect the settlement of St. Augustine in the early 1700s. **Right.** 1783 map of the 13 original American colonies. **Page 8. Inset.** Portrait of King James I by Circle of John de Critz, Circa 1600. **Page 11.** 1590 colored engraving by Theodore de Bry. The Town of Secota. Reproduced from the engraving made by John White, who witnessed the first colonization by the English in Virginia. White's portrayal shows a well-established society. The corn is in three stages of growth for three separate harvests. **Page 12. Inset.** Colonist with tobacco leaf. During a historical reenactment at Colonial Williamsburg, a man grades tobacco leaves. **Page 15. Top left.** Hand-colored woodcut circa 1790, shows Africans forced to march to the port or a market where they would be sold as slaves. **Bottom.** Original order for sale of African boy in 1761. Document owned by Mr. George Langdon of Plymouth, Connecticut. **Page 16. Top.** Early eighteenth-century view of Harvard, Stoughton, and Massachusetts Halls at Harvard College in Cambridge, Massachusetts, circa 1739. The college was founded in 1636 and grew up around Harvard Yard. **Inset.** *Boy with Squirrel* by John Singleton Copley. 1765. From the Museum of Fine Arts, Boston. **Page 19. Top.** Painting of the Pilgrims signing the Mayflower Compact, by Jean Leon Gerome Ferris, 1620. **Bottom.** Pilgrim signatures, circa 1620. Included are William Bradford, Myles Standish, and Edward Winslow. **Page 20.** Old New York City as Dutch colony Nieuw Amsterdam. 1625–1664.

Web Sites

Due to the changing nature of Internet links, PowerKids Press has developed an online list of Web sites related to the subject of this book. This site is updated regularly. Please use this link to access the list:

www.powerkidslinks.com/psima/coloam/